THE SADNESS WILL LAST FOREVER

THE SADNESS WILL LAST FOREVER

A Collection of Poetry

LUKE BARKER

BALBOA.
PRESS

A DIVISION OF HAY HOUSE

Balboa Press books may be ordered through booksellers or by contacting:

Balboa Press
A Division of Hay House
1663 Liberty Drive
Bloomington, IN 47403
www.balboapress.com
1 (877) 407-4847

Because of the dynamic nature of the Internet, any web addresses or
links contained in this book may have changed since publication and
may no longer be valid. The views expressed in this work are solely those
of the author and do not necessarily reflect the views of the publisher,
and the publisher hereby disclaims any responsibility for them.

The author of this book does not dispense medical advice or prescribe the use
of any technique as a form of treatment for physical, emotional, or medical
problems without the advice of a physician, either directly or indirectly. The
intent of the author is only to offer information of a general nature to help
you in your quest for emotional and spiritual well-being. In the event you use
any of the information in this book for yourself, which is your constitutional
right, the author and the publisher assume no responsibility for your actions.

Any people depicted in stock imagery provided by Thinkstock are
models, and such images are being used for illustrative purposes only.
Certain stock imagery © Thinkstock.

Print information available on the last page.

ISBN: 978-1-4525-2886-1 (sc)
ISBN: 978-1-4525-2887-8 (e)

Balboa Press rev. date: 05/11/2015

I dedicate this collection to the friends and family that have supported me through thick and thin times in my life. You guys prove to still come through for me in the end and I appreciate it greatly. I love you all so much and I hope that you enjoy what I have written. Some things may have you questioning whether I'm really okay or not but some of these poems express how I truly feel and experience through my schizophrenia. The others are just stories and ideas that I wish to share with the world. So again please enjoy my writings and let's hope and strive for a shining future. Thank you.

Butterfly & Moth

Wings of the dawn, A butterfly is born
Wings of the dusk, A moth is born

Flutter the butterfly goes, It breathes in life
Scatter the moth goes, It exhales death

Two forces of nature clash, An order to be kept
To step on one is punishable, We'll suffer never the less

As we care not for the two, They fly away from us
They have left us behind, Or have we just stopped caring?

Flutter butterfly, Scatter moth
Our time has come, For fate is all the same

Wings of dawn, Wings of dusk
We flutter at dawn, But we scatter at dusk

GENESIS

The sky has lost its colour
The sea is empty
The earth has lost its life
The animals begin to suffer
The humans to do the same
The end has begun
Or has the beginning finally arrived?
The world itself just a pebble
In the stepping stones of the universe
Making its mark in the galaxy
The Milky Way now reborn
We can finally breath in
And exhale opportunities
Of better lives and greater potentials
This is just the beginning of the story
In the ancient epic we call life
So take up arms and fight for tomorrow
For the dawn will come soon I promise
So lift your heads up high and hope for me
Hope that the suns light will reach you soon enough

HOW IT ENDS

The horse of red trots along the ground
The blood has stained the grass
The bodies of the fallen warriors pile on top of each other
War had landed.

The horse of black trots along the ground
People starve and people crave
Hunger and lust sink into their wounds
Famine has landed

The horse of white trots along the ground
Plagues follow with every breath exhaled
A loss of hope has risen
Conquest has landed.

The horse of pale trots along the ground
The spirit of hades rides alongside him
People drop one by one
Death has landed.

The four gather after years of exile
They chat of old stories from past events
They draw their weapons and charge
The apocalypse has started.

As the human race scream in terror, the world crumbles
The sky turns red and the oceans to black
I stand in the midst of the end and think to myself
"We as such flawed creatures deserve such a fate."

Touching Stars

Befallen around you are your old
surroundings of violence and disbelief
Broken through to the other side, a
new light burns within you
Now that your lighter than air you can see the stars
As they burn and prosper around you the smiles grow larger
The world is now a different place to be in.

A universe moves just for you so don't take it for granted
With the stars around you the future seems brighter
Don't fall back down to earth after making this far
Soar into a new galaxy and burn as the star you are
Burn star, burn.

The night sky is now naked without you.

THE VAMPIRE OPERA

The night is their domain
They are the eternal
Hundreds flock together
For the performance is about to begin

The music starts and the audience grows silent
These are sounds heard by no man before
Compositions crafted by the hands of monsters
Their sounds are lullabies to them

Tears have filled the eyes of the audience
The beauty of the music has reached their non-existent souls
They all realize that even monsters can be beautiful
There is beauty in all things

The opera has come to an end
The audience gives a standing ovation
Cheers fill the concert halls
Their dead hearts have been moved

The monsters want to coexist peacefully
But their mechanics have them feast for blood
Theses flawed creatures are too animalistic
Their desires are what make them tick

Monsters and humans are both animals in the end
The eternal struggle must come to an end soon
Both sides must learn that survival is life's ultimate goal
There is so much beauty within the beast

Skin

The kiss was that of death
It's cold embrace haunted the lips
The stinging lingered on the taste
From an apple red to a deep ocean blue
The lips now stained by the gentle touch of lips
Upon the reflection glass we call a mirror
His love for himself was enough to make you sick
The makeup, that of a whore
He looked too much like a women to have a dick
The pride in his complexion ruptured the soul
The boy, barely a man pouted in the mirror
He looks up over his head and stares deeply
Into the words scrapped into the glass
It screamed the word "VANITY"
The boy laughed and reapplied his lipstick
And then the beauty that stood before him turned sinister
Into that of a beast
The boy shocked by the image in front of him
He couldn't believe that the monster before him was himself
His soul finally baring its teeth to him
So swiftly he shatters the mirror into thousands
All broke except for the carving of the word "VANITY"
It stayed as a reminder of what kind of beast he really was
As the pieces finally finish raining as he drops dead
The glass had created too many incisions skin deep
He bled to death before the mirror had
finished breaking his soul
Lying dead on the floor his lips turn to a pure white

As if his soul was cleansed
But we all know that such a beast was
doomed from the beginning
I guess skin only shows so much but mirrors show the soul
Vanity took hold and created the beast within
Beauty didn't fall in love with the beast
Beauty killed the beast and died with it
So don't become either beauty or the beast
Stay who you are and love yourself
For I promise you that someone will love you
Not for what's on the skin
But rather what's under it
True beauty

A Body of Water

Sink into the pond
Sink into the river
Sink into the lake
Sink into the ocean

Sink into the eternity
Sink into the release
Sink into the weightlessness
Sink into the lifelessness

Sink into the body of water
Sink into the feeling of nothingness
Sink into the end of the world
Sink into the end of your very being

All that's left of the world is this
The body of water that we stand in
Take my hand and fall back into its depths with me
Let's sink together so that we're not so alone on the other side

CROW NOSE

I drew you into creation
You were my friend
Then you became my enemy
With my pen you gained breath
Now you wish to take breath away

With your own pen you draw a world within
It scares me and everyone else
Red lines turn into bloodshed
The innocent to run in fear
Only me to stand in your way

The pen, mightier than the sword
But our pens are our swords
Swiss and clang they clash
Your scared my enemy
But I'm here as a friend

Purple lines turn into salvation
Your lines turn into dust before your eyes
The world now in my hands
But you have already won
It's just us left in it now

My friends
My family
My lover
Gone from existence
Just us remain

You laugh in happiness
But you wanted my happiness
And I cry out for them
It scares you and kills you internally
Your wicked mask turns into ash

All I see now is the boy I left behind
A boy who already died
Now a man who won't let go of the past
A man who could've lived
But chose to dwell with your ghosts

I still hold the world in my hands
So I raise my pen one last time
And rewrite existence
But this time you don't get a life
You don't get an existence

Cry all you want but I need them more then you
My old friend
My deadly enemy
It's time to let the past go
It's time for a new world order

I shatter my pen and the world is reborn
In the palm of my hands new life exhales
But with life comes death
I look up to find that my old friend is gone
All that remains is a body with a sword through it

O' the Crow Nose
A boy who wanted to rule the world
But in the end died with it
Now a new world exudes out human nature
But how human was he anyway?

The rainbow now scattered into the wind
The memory of the artist along with it
But his inspiration lives on
I'll keep her safe I promise
Now that the world is a safer place

That's the problem when the world can be held in our hands
We'll do anything to reshape it in our image
But human nature is filthy
In the end it was an artist who created the world again
Just as god did years ago

THE SLEEP I LONG FOR BUT KNOW WON'T COME

Bats screech past my bedroom window
The sound of their wing beats haunt me
The lamp next to me burns like a candle
It flickers from the draft in the walls

The world outside my window is pitch black
Or is it the deep blue of the ocean?
Either way there's no way to navigate its depths
Who knows what lurks within the darkness

Creatures of the night move like shadows
As they are unable to be seen by my naked eye
I continue to stare out the window trying to spot one
But without any luck I retreat from
the glass back to my room

There before me are my familiar surroundings
A bed, a desk, that's all worth mentioning
Not enough but all that can fit with this room
A room that sometimes feels like a coffin

It's midnight again
And I just can't seem to fall asleep
Am I too full of energy maybe?
No, I know why I can't sleep

The chatter and gossip of voices in my head
High pitched laughs and unable to comprehend whispers
They become my very reason for all those sleepless nights
Just talking all night long

I find it hard to focus on anything else
I can't seem to drown them out so I sit in silence
I listen to them and fear that they won't talk about me
I'm scared for my sanity

The sun has risen and there goes another sleepless night
All the dreams I could've had now a fleeting idea
There is no hope for me if this is to be my fate every night
My eyes they long for the sweet embrace of unconsciousness

QUICKSAND

I've become stuck within
I can't seem to be able to break free
My feet are bound to this place
As I try to move I begin to sink

This quagmire has become my prison
My cries for help are unheard
I'm alone in this world
Or have I become theirs.

They surround me as they sink with me
They swim through the earth to reach me
They latch on and drag me down faster
They have become my very being

I have been engulfed by the quicksand
I lose my breath as darkness sets in
This to become my new surroundings
The company of hatred and love all in one

So call my name and cry for me
I have become lost in the quicksand
They have taken me for their own
And I don't know if I'm alive anymore

VERGLAS

I'm trapped within verglas
Unable to move at all
I don't know what's colder
The rock or the ice

I'm trapped within verglas
My breath freezing in my mouth
My body starts to collapse
My mind losing its sanity

I'm trapped within verglas
Hearts begin to weep for me
But don't you worry about me
I'm already too far gone

I'm trapped within verglas
My eyes to close fast
My heart to beat no more
I'm gone

THE GREED

What's yours is mine
What's mine is mine

Your life is mine for the taking
And so is mine

Your breath is mine
Your heart is mine

Your blood runs red
That's now mine

I love life so much
I wouldn't take mine

I'm too scared to lose it
So that's why I'll take yours

I take life for myself
To make it mine is my design

Life doesn't belong to anyone
I have no right to take it

But I'll still take it for myself
For my desire is strong

Mine, mine, mine
All mine

With a swift cut you bleed
And pour out sweet gold

I bathe my hands in it
To feel life force in the palms

As gold as it is
It's still too red for my liking

Let's spread around the love
Let's all pick up a knife

Let's all take life for ourselves
Let's take, take, take!

Take, take, take, take!
Let's take everything!

What's yours is mine
What's mine is mine

Let's take the world for ourselves
Let's, take... EVERYTHING!!!

THE KNIVES

They wear the faces of friends and family
Their eyes full of hatred
Their smiles so sinister
Their laughter so haunting

Illusions or visions of the future?
Hands covered in my blood
They hold their weapons high
They repeat the entries

All I see are the knives
This is why I don't sleep
The same dream over and over
Always with the same outcome

I drown in my own blood
They smile and laugh
The family are feeding
They feed on my tears

My sight grows blurry
My lungs full of blood
My eyes pouring tears
The family satisfied

I wake up
I stare at my ceiling
I roll over
Here goes another sleepless night

A Shiver of Sharks

I've cut my hand and now it's spilling in the water
The wound burns like the fires of hell
But that's not what I'm afraid of
But of the sharks that are now hunting my scent

I hear them cutting through the water like paper
With teeth sharp as rusted knives
And skin grey as storm clouds
They hunt in a shiver of sharks
Coming ever so closer

They reach my person and tear me apart
Limb by limb I lose them all
All is taken but my head
For that's their domain now
As they take hold and live on forever within

DEEP

Deep down in the corners of my mind
I find myself thinking
Of all the positives and negatives
That seem to break and mold me

Drowning into subconsciousness I find release
Deep down I want to be happy
But I can't do it alone
So that's why I call on you for my support

Sinking into weightlessness I find peace
Into the deep is where I'll go
To be one with the ocean is where I want to be
To be one with existence is to be free

Lungs filling up with air under water
I want you to love me for me
But I can't let you hate me too
So let me go and hope for a better tomorrow

Deep down in the organ we call "heart"
I come to realise that my happiness is what I want
So I'll continue on for years to come
And hope that I won't drown in the
depths of my ocean of a mind

THE DROWNER

Why do I have friends?
All I do is bring down the people close to me
Why do my family stay by my side?
When all I really am is a burden

They all care for me
That's what I'm told
But how can I believe anything they say
When it's just contradicted in my head

Whenever I sleep they talk to me
And it's always the same thing
Loneliness and death
Never anything new

Let me tell you a secret about my dreams
Every night I dream that I drown
They hold me under and I try to surface
But in the end I always fall into the depths of the ocean

I try to stay afloat all the time
But as it would seem I'm not a good swimmer
Especially when I'm weighed down by the voices
It's as the song speaks for me

In all my dreams I drown
The lyrics of the song become my story
Etched into my brain and soul
I am living proof that I'm a drowner

What could I possibly dream of instead?
Fame?
Fortune?
Love?

As much as I would love them they are out of reach
I am my own worst enemy
With a family that live in my head
No one would want me

It's dark where I am
The bubbles are my bed
As they drag my down
I become one with my nightmares

I scream but no one hears me
All I do is let water fill my lungs
My sight grows blurry
And my mind slows down

I am the drowner
And I'll be drowning for the rest of my life
Someone please raise my to the surface
For I am not a good swimmer

LOST AT SEA

I am so lost at sea
My boat is getting fuller everyday
My family and I sail on these high seas
Hoping to find a place of peace
But these storm ridden waters trap us
And soon we'll capsize due to our weight

The waves crash into us so hard
I lose my footing all the time
But I haven't fallen out yet
My family hold onto me ever so tightly
They don't want to lose me just yet
But soon enough I'll be going overboard

I have fears that the boat will get too heavy
I have fears that I'll truly be lost when I fall into the water
I don't know if me falling in is what my family wants
If I fall in then I'll be theirs for eternity
But if I stay on this boat I'll lose myself in the crashing waves
What do they really want from me is the mystery here

I just want to be free of all this
But how can I be free when I'm stuck here
Stuck on a tiny boat with a large family
Their voices haunt me and kill me internally
I just want release
Is that too hard to ask for?

The boat starts to rock and the waves take us under
My family latch onto me and I start to drown
I'm being dragged down into the dark blue depths
I guess this is what they wanted
For us to die as the family we are
I am now truly lost at sea

ADRIFT AT SEA

I am adrift at sea
Sinking deep into the abyss
My family drag me into nothingness
Their smiles linger in my eyes
The bubbles escape from my lungs
I'm losing my reason to be

Schools of fish swim past
All the colors of the rainbow shimmer before me
They fill me with a calming feeling
A sense of acceptance of my fate
As I try to touch them they scatter
A shiver of sharks approaches

Their color is a confronting grey
My rainbow has vanished
And now it seems that death's color has taken form
They race toward and circle us
I feel the cold embrace of death on my shoulder
These sharks are his welcoming party

I attempt to scream but all I do is lose more air
Just ensuring death that I'll be at his door soon enough
I shut my mouth and gaze at my family
as they continue to smile
The sharks are what they want
To assure that we die as a family and not apart
Their grip on me tightens and we begin to sink faster

Amongst the madness I recollect my thoughts and memories
This is truly the end?
Will death be a comforting companion?
How much more air do I have before I truly drown?
These thoughts haunt me and fill me with terrors
The ocean blue around me slowly turns to black

As we begin to enter uncharted waters
I study my surroundings
The creatures that dwell within the darkness
frighten me more than death
How could such things survive without
the warmth of the sun?
The creatures keep their distance as if I am contaminated
I guess they fear what they don't understand
Such is human nature

My vision grows blurry and darkness settles in
My family and the sharks continue to linger with me
I hit solid ground and I lay on the
ocean floor staring skyward
I can't see anything anymore
I guess that's what happens when you give up hope
You soon realize that there's no light
at the bottom of the ocean

I can't even tell if my family or the sharks are still by my side
I reach upward and grasp onto nothing
My breath almost gone my body begins to shut down
My eyes begin to close and I'm embraced by more darkness
My new surroundings scare me but I
feel like this what I deserve
I am truly now adrift at sea

FOUND AT SEA

Eternity has passed it seems since I capsized
The darkness around still holds me tight
I can hear the faint sound of whispers
My family speak to me one last time before I pass
They utter words of torment and fill me with memories
My life starts to flash before my closed eyes

They show me from the first whisper to now
The pain I've endured in my lifetime
The pills and alcohol I've consumed
seem to be a far off dream
They show me my friends and family
Will they miss me?
Or will they be relieved that I'm finally gone?

My skin is as cold as death's breath
I can't move any part of my body anymore
I think the end has finally come into effect
My lungs have no air left in them at this point
My body has truly taken the weight
that is my family of voices
I feel the warm embrace of sharks' teeth on my icy skin

The whispers grow deafening as the sharks begin to feast
They are truly happy now that we will all be together forever
If I could shed a tear I would
I would cry because I would've liked to have
tried to make my life worth something
Try to fight back but in the end I gave in and drowned
I guess I wasn't a good swimmer after all

As the whispers begin to fade into non-
existence I hear something new
Something more than a whisper
I hear people crying and shouting from a distance
My fingers begin to twitch and the
teeth of the sharks disappear
My eyes feel a warm embrace as they come back to life
I open them slightly and I see what appears to be light

I was shocked to the sight
Did death take me and this is the afterlife?
I assumed it wasn't due to the newly gained
energy I was receiving from the light
I stared deep into its vastness and not once blink
The more I continued to stare the more
the new voices became coherent
These new voices were not foreign but familiar

"Don't give up!"
"Come back to us please!"
"We love you so much!"
I couldn't believe what I was hearing
These were the voices of the friends and family I left behind
Why are they calling out to me?

My body no longer felt heavy and I
start to move around more
The light has illuminated me enough for me
to see my own hands raised above me
They stand tall aiming skyward and wanting
the embrace of the new voices
I drop my hands and stare back into the
light that has given me new life
Was this light my savior?
Or is just a trick from the family to get me to hope again?

I pondered the thoughts for what
seemed to be another eternity
As I laid there staring up all I could hear were
the kind words that want me home
The family the dwell in my mind were
nowhere to be found and I was scared
I've gone without them harassing me
before and then was cut down hard
What will be different this time to
make them not come back?
I thought of just staying here in the
darkness forever to avoid the pain

"They will always there but that doesn't
mean you have to live in fear"
"Learn to coexist and fight them with a stronger conviction"
"Don't give up when you still got a whole life ahead of you"
Their words louder than ever really touched my heart
Maybe I could learn to fight back for once and actually win
Maybe they have a point

I noticed around me hiding in the darkness
were the family and the sharks
They kept their distance as if the light would burn them
My lungs now regaining air again I sigh
and hold my hand out to them
"Come, together we can live as one"
The family horrified hesitated to reach for my hand
They were scared of my newly gained confidence

I dived into their eyes with mine and they spoke to them
My eyes now filled with hope burned
them from the inside out
They all cried out in pain as I took hold of them all
Huddled together my body slightly
raises from the ocean floor
Somehow I feel lighter even with them still holding me down
We begin to leave the darkness behind
and rise into open water

I looked down to see the shiver of sharks
harboring within the darkness below
They start to vanish before my eyes as I begin to realize
I won't be seeing death for years to come
The color of blue surrounds me once again
The rainbow I once saw what seemed to
be a lifetime ago has reappeared
It shined with new ideas and realizations

Faster and faster we begin to surface
The light now growing in size as it
touches everything around me
It burns pure hope into my tortured soul
The family start to merge with my being as
we grow ever so closer to the surface
I have become both heavier and lighter
I smile and in a flash I'm breathing in fresh air

I try to stay afloat as I scan the horizons for land
I hear cheering behind me and I turn to find a ship
Aboard were all my friends and family
waiting to welcome me back
They throw out a life preserver and I take hold
Slowly but surely I'm dragged through
the waves and onboard
I am met with smiles and warm embraces

As I am being hugged ever so tightly I begin to hear whispers
The family have surfaced in the tides of my mind
I smile and laugh at their attempts to terrorize me
I have come to realize that I am to be
tormented by them for years to come
Its how I choose to fight that will decide the victor
And I'm letting them know now, I won't die defeated

The winds take hold of our sails and
we carry onward to shore
I watch the ocean vigilantly as I remember
that I could end up back here one day
I will never be sailing alone on these high seas
As long as I have my friends and family
I won't be defeated so easily
I close my eyes and take in the light of the sun
I have be found at sea

Tragedian

Basked in tragedy, I am
The curtain rises but I hear no applause
Why am I left to face life alone?

Centre stage I stand
The gods to despise me
He who has been forgotten

I am a thespian
He who is given stories to re-enact
But I'm living the saddest story ever told

The solitude
The feeling of being alone kills me
Yet I love it too

This aspect of death is choking me
The grip it has around my neck
I don't want to die alone

We're born alone and die alone
It's just the inevitable truth of life
That this feeling is what kills us

Loneliness
It feeds on us
It preys on the weak

The act ends and so does the play
Life to come to its proper demise
We as a species to go with it

I'm trying my best to hold on dearly
But there's not enough to hold on to
I've lost my footing, I've lost the ability to breath

So my eyes close softly
And darkness takes hold
My lungs they have no vitality

Life force a distant thought
And now we close the pages on this epic
And begin the next chapter

Basked in tragedy I am
The curtains fall and there's still no applause
Life is now a fleeting memory

CALAMITY

I'm falling into the atmosphere at a
speed that can't be measured
Will I burn up and scatter into thousands of pieces?
Or will I hit the earth with such an impact
that it'll change human nature?
I guess no one really knows what will
happen until the future hits us

The past seems so real and it hurts still but
hopefully it'll fade away properly
The future is so close to happening you can
see the light of it shinning before you
I want things to happen and un-happen but
I can't change or make it happen faster
All we can do is wait for it to happen
and be stuck with it forever

Falling from space into the exosphere feels like
this and the burning is the constant reminder
The past burns us but only we can put out
the fires that cause all this harm
As much as I want to change what has
happened I cannot so I fall
I fall into the thermosphere and become
the future that I've been waiting for

Faster and faster I fall it seems that
I'll end life on earth this way
The mesosphere welcomes me and open
my eyes to embrace the future
It shines so bright that I begin to cry from what I see
Am I happy with what has happened or am I full of regret?

I know what I want in my future and
it will be what I'll strive for
Am I crying because you're in it as what I want?
Or am I no longer a part of your life?
The stratosphere takes me in as I continue to
plummet through the atmospheres of earth

The troposphere has become my surrounding
as I make my final descent to earth
I am the calamity that'll either end life or ensure the future
But no one will know until it happens
So this serves as my lesson to live by

Ensure to strive for your goals and dreams or
they float away and become naught
Fall into the future and learn from
your mistakes and memories
Even if she's not my lover in the end she'll still be my friend
And that's when I hit the earth and then all I hear is silence

AFTERMATH

The world has ended
I lay in the crater I created
All I smell is ash
All I hear is nothing

The sky is vermillion
The clouds are the deepest of black
I caused this destruction
I am the reason that life has ended

I stand up and climb out of the crater
The earth around me comes into sight
The debris haunts me
The pile of corpse's tower high

I shed a tear for humanity
All I wanted was to learn from my past
All I wanted was to embrace the future
But all I did was send life to the reaper

I was trying to forget the pain of my past
I wanted something new to hold onto
But in the end I fell and wiped out existence
All I wanted was a lover

She hurt me in a millisecond of my fall
She tried to make me understand her pain
But I turned away and left her alone
In the end I felt like the enemy that hurt us

All she did was try to make me realize us
That we weren't right for each other
Better off as friends
But I didn't want friendship, I wanted a relationship

She never meant to hurt me
I never meant to act the way I did
Emotions can make a man act irrationally
And for that I am sorry

I begin to walk away from ground zero
The ash covered earth immortalizes the fallen
The memories of the past begin to haunt me
My tears burn my cheek as they run down them

I still want the future
I'm sick of the pain of the past
Its ghosts have haunted me enough
It's time to move on

I wipe away the tears and stare up at the sun
Its brightness is fading away but I hope for its return
I don't want to lose her
I need her in my life

I sit down on the ash covered earth
I take a handful of it and let it run through my fingers
To me it tells me that time is fleeting
And I have to make the best of what I'm given

I begin to smile and laugh at memories of her
She was a part of my life
She was stranger that grew into a treasured friend
I can't let her go

I need her
Even if she isn't my lover she'll still be my friend right?
Does she hate me or does she think I hate her?
I have forgotten and moved on and I hope we can too

The world has ended and I'm alone again
But with her as my friend I'll never be truly alone
I want her to know that I'm sorry even
if an apology isn't needed
I want you as my friend if that's okay with you?

I know life will return
So let's wait for it together
Let's make history
Will you still be my friend even on this destroyed planet?

The silence has broken and all I hear is
the future forming around us

GENUINE SUICIDE

The girl leaking tears over memories
The kind of things that keep you up at night
Those sleepless nights that turn into nightmares
The images of self-loathing and being hated

The girl hates this world and wants to leave it
Pills and booze go down smoothly at first
But after a while it all goes downhill from there
Being found unconscious in a bathroom at home

The girl now at hospital being saved from her overdose
She comes back to life but then realises
that she's still breathing
The hysterics and screams haunt the halls of the wing
She looks up to the nurse and speaks at last

"Why did you save me? I don't want to be here."
"Why did you save me? There's no point in living"
The nurse breaks into tears as we come to realise
That this has been a most genuine suicide.

THE GHOST & HAMLET

The villain and his child
One born into crime and the other built around it
Do we feel sorry for the man with the gun?
Or the child who holds the knife?

The villain
A man who was born as this
To become the man he is today
The killer he is now

The child
Built into a weapon
Innocence is killed
Violence sets in

The villain born into crime
The child to become crime itself
A king and a prince
Ruling over dirt and grime

The villain to be gunned down
Justice sweeps through him
Blood covering the pavement
So ends the villain

The prince now a king
Hamlet to kill Claudius
Claudius is justice
And Hamlet is crime

Dirt and grime never looked better
As the king now is a father
So continues the cycle of born and built
Now the king realising he was born for crime

As his child is now built into a prince
The prince of crime
His crown the bones of his enemies
As Claudius soon falls by his sword

27 & OTHER NUMBERS

Their ghosts hang on our walls in the
form of paper and cardboard
Their faces, a reminder of the past and
how much of a simpler time it was
Their names live on as a legacy of the
good and bad they've done
Their lives have touched us in ways
they wouldn't have dreamed of

Their words live on as inspiration and
poetry to younger generations
Their legend, a ripple in the pool of life
Their music was and still is the subject of
debate whether it's the best or not
Their memory will be cherished from time to come

The club they belong to is exclusive and
only accepts certain applicants
The fame and fortune needed is that of the gods
But who wants to stay the age twenty seven forever
When all it brings to the world is sadness and misery

To think of what they could have done for the world
The foundations of their work created what we have today
Twenty seven immortalised forever in the cosmos
But people die at other numbers too

They became a world changing phenomenon
These people will forever be immortal in our eyes
Even though they're gone from our lives
They are and will be the gods we worship today

The gods of music

Swimming Until Tomorrow Comes

Horizons come closer
As I swim toward it
But then I realise that I don't swim well
So I begin to drown
Struggling to keep afloat I gasp for air
But all I do is swallow in the sea

Deep down I go
Passing schools of fish
I watch the past swim on by
But here I am drowning in the present
Without any sight of the future to come

Now I find the ocean floor
Oh how I become one with it and take in the world
My surroundings start to cave in on me
But it's okay
Because I think I might float again
Back up to the surface soon enough

I start to rise off the sand and begin my ascension
Up through the present days and into new dawns light
Kicking and pushing, I break through
and make it to the surface
And that's when I see the horizon ever so close now
So I begin to swim again hoping for the sun to never set

Cutting through and against the currents
I make it into new light
Oh how I bask in it now
So this is me lifting out of the water and now flying upwards
Into skies unknown but that's okay
For I believe that the day will treat me well
So the night will be ever so pleasant

ALWAYS AND FOREVER

Always and forever I fall as an anchor
For the fact is I'm losing breath

When the light in the eyes fades away
And turn into a milky colour of death
Your lungs start to shrink in size
Your heart starts to beat less and less
Your brain starts to lose its memories
And your whole being breaks down

You try to find the courage to carry on
But you notice that no one seems to care
So you drop down to quiver in fear
For you realise that your alone in the world
No one left around you to depend on

To be buried in the depths of the sea
Is a calming nature to me
As I begin to drift in and out of consciousness
I drown into the abyss of the ocean
The sharks to feed on me
This is the fate I've chosen

Sinking and sinking and sinking
This is the end
Believe me I have no regrets
This is the way I want it to be
To be beneath the waves is where I lay

So dry your tears and face new fears
The day isn't over for your yet
There's still tomorrow left to face
I let your hand go and sway with the rip tides
I am the undertow now
Laying here on the floor of the briny blue sea

The sounds of passing tides eases my body
As I always and forever lay here as the sand of the sea

SEASICK

In sickness and in health
Till death parts our ways
Searching over grey ocean skies
We are looking for ourselves
In the reflections of waters below

From side to side
Forwards and backwards
And upside down and back upside
We sway with the breeze as it hits our lungs
And fills us with dreams and desires

Our stomachs churn and bubble
To sounds of waves hitting bodies in the water
So hold on tight and don't let go
For there will be turbulence
On this ride we call life

In a way were all seasick
Being pushed backwards and forwards
By the seas of life
And when it's too much to handle anymore
Let it all flow from you and become one with all

The Lovely Siren Song

Would you kill yourself because you
love something so much?
The water now a colour of blood
But it stays blue in saturation
The creature now dying in its natural surroundings
Her tail has lost its feeling
Her breasts now shrivelling in size
Her hair turning to grey
The knife in her hand now her demise
She should have killed her love
But now her obsession has gotten the best of her
Blue blood of the mermaid
O' how it complements the sea
The sharks to feast upon her corpse
The fish to mourn their friend
What's left of her to sinks into the trenches
She becomes one with the sand
The knife floats though
Stained by the blood of her throat
The man she loved finds it washed upon the shore
He ponders the history of the weapon
Not knowing that it was to slay him
All for the purpose of love

But the emotion got the better of the creature
Now her song of love and loss will be sung
Future sirens will learn from this day
And that is how the sirens came to be
Their wicked ways now speak for the past
For one's obsession can kill
So beware the song at sea
For you might end up the same as the creature
In a shark filled graveyard beyond the reaches of sunlight
Down, down, down

At bottom of the sea

GOD HELP US NOW

My compass doesn't point north anymore
It's lost its way just as I have
Now here we are lost in the middle of a storm
That's ripping holes in the ocean
God help us now

In need of an asylum harbour we sail on
Through the waves as a high as a tower
They crash on top of us bringing us closer to hell
We start to drown on the deck of the ship
God help us now

The wind picks up and leads us through
But I'm afraid the sails will fail
As the typhoon hits us we all fall down
As our sails whisk us away to no man's land
God help us now

Waves crash against the bow and we lose footing
Over board and into the deep I go
Sinking down and being pushed around
My vision fades and I begin to lose breath
God help us now

I open my eyes wide after the storm has eased
I find myself surrounded by white and black
I feel the ocean touch me ever so slightly
I turn to god's face and say
"God help us now"

I'm stuck in an echo of my former self
As I lift off the ground and see nothing but the sea
I know where I am now
In the jaws of a watery grave
God, you haven't helped me at all

Love and Sirens

I'm in search of the sirens song
To be whisked away into bliss
Before I meet the sting of her tongue
I want to be in harmony with life
This is the way to live a life out at sea

High and low I search for her
From shorelines where the waves crash
To the swirling whirlpools that eat ships
I look with haste as if my time is coming to an end
But for all I know it may be

I've swallowed too much sea water
I think I'm going crazy
I'm hearing voices and speaking in tongues
My crew mates keep their distances
To avoid being near me

So that's why I look for her
Even though she'll send me to heaven
Before she sends me to hell
I yearn for her sight and kiss
For I am alone in this world

But maybe when I do find her she'll look past death
And see me for who I am and learn to love
That's the life for me
But alas I need a miracle for that to be more than a dream
So here's to dreaming of a sirens song

I put my life on the line as I sail with or without my crew
Just to hear the song of the end
But for I know it could be the beginning
to something beautiful
Or I could be dead by morning for all we know
These are the things we risk in search for love

But with a struck of luck I open my ears and hear something
It's sound was that of a cherub singing
for god to help him sleep at night
So I sail into its echoes and there I find her
The very siren I have been yearning for since dawns light
And now my journey has come to its end

I exit my ship and step towards her engaged by the sound
Her song so alluring it hurts
I make my penultimate step and reach her
Oh how her beauty amazes me
Now to see if I have bitten off more than I can chew

In an instant we embrace our lips and I feel everything
Like if the whole world was within this kiss
And as I lean out of it I fall backwards into the water
To live out the last moments of my life
For her sting was enough to kill me

I die with a smile on my face
Knowing that I have experienced love
So now I say to these my final words
So listen in close
For I don't have much time

The sting of the siren hurts even in the happiest of times
So follow her song and see what happens
For it may be different for you but for me it's over
But I die loving life and come to peace with myself
So mourn and listen to her song for its different for everyone

THE THRONE

O' death
Outside of space
Outside of time
You are the oldest

O' death
Your children now ready
They long for your attention
It's time to choose your heir

O' death
Your children are young
Their minds in different places
Are they worthy?

O' death
The fifth born, Bram
Hatred for living things
Can he bare the crown?

O' death
The fourth born, Libitina
An incestuous whore
Can she bare the crown?

O' death
The third born, Farren
An alcoholic
Can he bare the crown?

O' death
The second born, Parthenope
A killer of humans
Can she bare the crown?

O' death
The first born, Orestes
A manipulative tactician
Can he bare the crown?

O' death
The truth hurts
Your children are vile creatures
They have no right to rule

O' death
You decided to choose a human to crown
A young man to take the name
The eternal name of Daethus

O' death
Your children to oppose your decision
They are the rightful heirs
For they bare the true Daethus blood

O' death
You've made your choice
Now human blood courses through them
You hope this will change their ways

O' death
Your children to kill the human
A battle raged on earth
Tearing it asunder

O' death
You weep for the human race
A corrupt yet beautiful race
There aren't any left now

O' death
You feel this to be your fault
Earth has become a wasteland of souls
Each one going to the gates or the pit

O' death
Your children return to you
They bare fangs ready to attack
Patricide courses through their minds

O' death
It saddens you to lose your children
But they must be put down
For they will destroy the universe

O' death
Their blood is on your hands now
You weep for your fallen offspring
But knew that it was the right thing to do

O' death
You now sit upon your throne
You look upon the earth and mourn
There is no hope for the planet

O' death
Now alone in the universe
You are still the oldest
Older than god himself

O' death
I mourn for you
You've lost too much today
And gained no heir

O' death
Is it your time to go?
Where does death go to die?
Can you even die?

O' death
You are the end itself
The inevitable of existence
This has become your end

O' death
I am to go with you
For I am apart of you too
The voice in your head

O' death
I guess your schizophrenic
But I'm not against you
But rather with you

O' death
I love you
I want nothing but your happiness
But you just can't stop crying

O' death
I think it's time to go
But please answer me what I've already asked
How does death die?

O' death
I can feel your life force fade now
I to go with it
Goodnight dear king

O' death
The noble king
Unbiased
Sleep now and dream for eternity

LOVE(LESS)

Love
Why do we crave the chemicals?
Why do we starve for the companionship?
Why do put our hearts on the line for it?
I want answers but know I won't get any
I'll just continue to hurt myself

I started to notice girls at thirteen
The idea of having a lover was exciting
Someone to hold you close
Someone to kiss your lips
Someone to lean on in the darkest days
O how I yearned for it

A string of lovers over the years of adolescence
From one to another I continued to get hurt
The first was something special
It has made me think that no one can be trusted
She left me for another
Why was she with me if in the end she chose another?

After her, my heart felt like a black hole
Engulfing all hope for survival
But in the end I opened my heart up again
Only to have to ripped out more
I was slowly bleeding out
The sad thing is I'm still bleeding

I've broken a couple of hearts
But I was hurting more than they were
I had my reasons for ending the time we spent together
But they were either barely there or grew selfish
Then I continued onward alone
As I was from the beginning I will stay the same in the end

Negativity chokes me tight
I lose breath easily
I try to stay positive but what's the point?
Why try to love when you'll just end up hurt?
Either a loss of relationship or death occurs
The end will always end up in heartache

I think I'll just stay alone
Even with voices haunting me I'm not alone
Mentally I won't be but I will be physically
I'm sick of the anguish
People will try to make pursue happiness
But maybe I can be happy without a lover

To my dear lovely ghosts
The memories of you all will stay with me for years to come
You will continue to hurt and inspire me
Haunt and spook me to breaking point
It will serve as reminder that love is pointless
It's just chemical reactions after all

Loveless
Maybe I'll find someone to love me for me
To accept my flaws and positive qualities
But dreams have a tendency to not come true
So I'll just stay broken and alone for that's my fate
I'll accept the loneliness and not be anyone's lover

SOMAH

I write these words so that maybe one
day you might read them
I want you to understand my pain
I need you to see what I saw
I cherish those memories fondly

You came into my life so suddenly
From a simple glance at me you began to emote
Feelings of young love soon swept through your mind
And soon enough you had swayed mine

Our simple like grew to powerful love
The time we spent together was priceless
If I could relive those memories I would
It was a simpler time when you were around

Every time we kissed my heart skipped a beat
Every time we held hands my soul would shake
You had such a spell over me I thought we would last forever
But sadly it came to an end one memorable winter

As the air grew icy so did your heart
You broke me into pieces that I couldn't recover
You chose not to do it face to face hurt the most
Through a screen was the way you chose to end it

Years later I found out you left me for another
It hurt but yet I still wanted to be a part of your life
But you shut me out and barely spoke to me
So eventually I lost you and now my heart aches

We meet in the summer as was your name
I'll hold you forever in my heart for years to come
Maybe our paths may cross again
Until then please smile the way you
use to when I said I loved you

The Devil and His Riches

I stole beauty today
The grace of the devil
Wings that shone with everlasting light
I raided the devil of his riches

It's not like he needs it anymore
Where he is there's no need for light
Only the abyss that the darkness of hell
Not fire, just everlasting darkness

Darkness that just engulfs all
Not leaving any trace of purity
In a hell like that
Why does he need grace?

As I try to leave the dark place I'm confronted
The seducer himself stood in front of me
All his beauty gone, nowhere to be seen
The rage he exuded was unfathomable

He offered a deal as he would
His grace for everlasting life
I pondered the thought of eternity
But I decided against it

I told him that what I held in my hands must be returned
Returned to its maker to be loved once again
Then the Devil wept in the memory of his love
For his father and his beauty

I guess we just don't understand the creature that is Satan
For all we know he could be repenting his sin
And god couldn't care less if his beloved Lucifer is crying
Crying for his father to forgive his mistakes

As I watched the creature weep I feel pain for my actions
So I decided to return what I had stolen
I placed the grace in his hands and left
I don't think I have ever felt so sorry for anything in my life

As I return to heaven and speak with my
father I tell him of my thoughts
God hated what I had done for he believes
that we as humans are pure
Because we are able to make decisions
without God watching over us
And that his child told him for that because
of that design we are flawed

So I told him that the beauty of men is
nothing compared to the Devil's
For he can weep and feel sorry for his
actions as a seducer of evil
Our grace is corrupted
Or maybe his tears were that of the liar he is depicted as

The truth is I don't know who to side with anymore
The creator or the betrayer
Either way I know something that we should be aware of
Grace is fleeting, beauty isn't as deep as you think
when even evil looks so good sometimes

I stole beauty today and it's gone forever.

Printed in the United States
By Bookmasters